Great British Pub Dogs

FROM DACHSHUNDS TO GREAT DANES, THE CANINE RESIDENTS OF BRITAIN'S PUBS

ABBIE LUCAS & PAUL FLECKNEY

ROBINSON

First published in Great Britain in 2017
by Robinson

Copyright © Abbie Lucas & Paul Fleckney,
2017

10 9 8 7 6 5 4 3 2 1

The moral right of the authors has been
asserted.

A CIP catalogue record for this book is
available from the British Library.

ISBN 978-1-47213-917-7

Papers used by Robinson are from well-
managed forests and other responsible
sources.

Typeset in Whitman & Adelle Sans

Designed by Andrew Barron @ thextension

Printed and bound in China by
C&C Offset Printing Co, Ltd

Robinson
An imprint of
Little, Brown Book Group
Carmelite House, 50 Victoria Embankment,
London EC4Y 0DZ

An Hachette UK Company

www.hachette.co.uk

www.littlebrown.co.uk

Preface

We met old dogs, new dogs, bilingual and three-legged dogs. We met the horse-sized, the pint-sized, and the blind in one eye.

We met dogs named after philosophers, footballers and *Coronation Street* characters. Dogs named after Japanese films stars and the Hungarian credit crunch.

Dogs who'd met a Beatle, dogs who'd met a Clooney, dogs so cute you could hardly walk away from them (Rudi, we're looking at you).

Some of them had been in the wars: locked in a shed, hit by a van, had acid thrown over them. Now they have new careers as pub dogs – fresh starts in loving homes.

We met a clan of three Jack Russells, a gang of four red setters. A bulldog who spun like a ballerina, a whippet who buried custard creams, a bichon frise who didn't let you leave.

There were dogs who attended pub meetings, dogs who lived on a roof. Top-heavy dogs who fell in canals, bear-like dogs who nicked sticks off kids.

Then there were the adventure dogs, who went canoeing and cross-country skiing. And the ones who stayed at home, forever by the fire, or beneath the plate of sausage rolls.

When we embarked on the Pub Dogs project in 2010, we never thought we would uncover such a startling range of breeds, personalities and stories. About the only thing that united them was how well loved they were by the pub customers. There were countless tales of how people came in especially to visit the dog, enjoy its company, maybe even take it for a walk. In the words of one of the locals at the Crown Inn, Axbridge: 'He [Dexter] was more of a friend than a dog.' A pub dog is quite simply a civic asset.

And yet, even in the course of compiling this book, six of the dogs have died, and several of the pubs have closed down (a sadly common trend). So what you see in *Great British Pub Dogs* is a transient slice of British culture, a snapshot in time. Pubs are there to be used, pub dogs are there to be appreciated. Some of these dogs are even the recipients of our special awards, such as the 'Lifetime Achievement Award', 'Most Charismatic Award' and the much-coveted 'Top Pub Dog Award', plus one town has been crowned 'Pub Dog Capital of Britain' (look out for the award icons throughout the book).

Thanks to everyone who tipped us off about the dogs, online or off. Thanks to everyone who put us up on our travels, gave us lifts and helped us in any way. We hope you enjoy the book.

1 Monty

GREAT BRITISH PUB DOGS

Name Monty

Breed Jackhuahua (Jack Russell and chihuahua cross)

Age Six

Owners Bruce and Sally Thomson

Monty in three words Cute, affectionate, 'frisky'.

Named after French philosopher Michel de Montaigne, whose works Sally was reading when she got him. One of Montaigne's central theories was that the best things happen by accident, which is exactly how Monty and Sally came together.

Loves Being cuddled, and young children (he was raised by a child who dressed him like a child and put him in a pram, so he loves being with five- to seven-year olds now).

Hates Postmen. This includes off-duty postmen having a quiet pint.

Favourite toy His little rabbit, and a tiny ball which is the exact size of his mouth, so he can grip it, but can't drop it.

Special move Standing on his back legs, dancing around looking like a meerkat.

Favourite food Rump steak.

Favourite spot in the pub Sally's lap. He also has a seat in the corner of the lounge bar.

Love interest Tilly, a Jack Russell who visits from Cornwall. He follows her, enraptured, copying her, doing things he isn't normally brave enough to do, like diving into rivers.

Best friend Prince, another Jackhuahua who lives opposite the nearby Cobweb Hall.

Key info Monty was one of eight very pretty dogs, but had short legs, a big head and a huge tail. The other puppies bullied him, so he developed a personality instead.

Pub nugget #1 The inn dates back to a staggering 1282.

Pub nugget #2 The Highwayman Inn is known for being one of the UK's most eccentric pubs. The features Sally has installed include a wishing tree, a crystal tree, a Tutankhamun statue, a dragon on the roof that breathes 'fire', a 6ft minotaur and a grotto section.

Pub nugget #3 Sally's father was the previous owner and took the pub in its unusual direction. He built a section of the pub to look like the inside of a ship's hull, using materials from a whaling boat called *Diana*, which was shipwrecked in Greenland in 1866, with nineteen of the crew dying of scurvy. The ship was freed and towed back, but broke up on Donna Nook in Lincolnshire, one of Britain's most treacherous bits of coastline.

2 Shiraz

EAST DART HOTEL, POSTBRIDGE, DEVON

Name Shiraz

Breed Black Newfoundland

Age Nine

Owners Paul and Rosie Joynson

Shiraz in three words Big, lazy, lovable

Weight 74kg (11½ stone).

Loves Being around people. She'll happily spend all day sitting next to people in the pub. She is intuitive with elderly or disabled people, watchfully waiting until they're settled before going to say hello.

Hates Anyone trying to sit on her back.

Favourite place to walk The woods near the River Dart, where he paddles.

Best doggie friends A collie called Archie and a Bedlington cross terrier called Yogi who belong to a barmaid at the hotel.

Special move Lying on her back and paddling her paws like she's riding a bike.

Scare story When she was a puppy living in Jersey, she and a friend were playing in the sea when a freak wave came in and washed over them. Now she doesn't go in water above her furry knees.

Claim to fame Shiraz appeared in *Griff's Great Britain* presented by Griff Rhys Jones. They were filmed walking around nearby Tavistock together. When the cameras

weren't rolling, one lady asked Griff to move so she could get a photo of Shiraz.

Pub nugget The pub claims to have inspired Arthur Conan Doyle to write *Hound of the Baskervilles*. He was staying at the nearby Laughter Hole House when he wrote it, and it's said that he found out about the legend of a fearsome dog – which inspired the book – from the landlord of the East Dart.

3 Guinness

NEW INN AT CROSS, SOMERSET

LIFETIME
ACHIEVEMENT
AWARD

Name Guinness

Breed Cocker spaniel

Age Twelve

Owners Steven Gard and Emma Britton

Guinness in three words Persistent, friendly, stout.

Best buddies A border collie called Jess, and a springer/collie called Desmond.

Favourite walking spots Kings Wood and Crook Peak, both nearby. The landlord's mother comes in most days to walk him.

Favourite food He's on a strict vegetarian diet as the pub dog lifestyle was taking its toll. It turns out he has a taste for cucumber and red pepper.

Loves When a regular comes in. He senses their arrival even when he seems to be asleep. In his younger days he would go flying across the slidy floors to greet them.

Favourite spot The fireplace when the fire isn't on because of the cold slabs, or, if no one's looking, the leather sofa.

Pub nugget The pub dates back to the 1600s as a coaching house. It's claimed that in the seventeenth century, prisoners who'd been sentenced to death by the famous 'hanging Judge Jeffreys' were held at the pub before being taken up nearby Wavering Down to the gallows.

4 Dexter

CROWN INN, AXBRIDGE, SOMERSET

'Local children sometimes stole him from the pub garden to play with him.'

Name Dexter (nickname Jabba the Mutt)

Breed Rottweiler (half Belgian Rottweiler, hence his larger size)

Time in pub 2008–16, he died aged nine

Owner Linda Bishop

The story behind the name He was going to be called Zac, but an eccentric old man in the pub, who'd been hitting the cider quite hard that day, said that the dog had told him he wanted to be called Dexter. Despite the man's unorthodox methods, Linda conceded the name was strong.

Dexter in three words Gentle, entertaining, loving.

Pub dog technique Dexter liked to climb on to the bench next to a customer, or even a group of people, and lean in for a cuddle. Local children sometimes stole him from the pub garden to play with him.

Favourite spot If the pub was quiet, Dexter would lie by the bar facing the front door. In the garden he liked to sit on one of the tables so he could be high up. 'He was a guard dog without being trained into it.'

Loves Being cuddled.

Hates Fireworks, drones, the moon and hot air balloons (which made the annual Bristol International Balloon Fiesta tricky). Also, burglars.

Key quote From one local, posted on Facebook after Dexter died: 'He was more of a friend than a dog.'

Pub nugget The building dates back to the fourteenth century as a medieval hall, and two of the original walls are still standing.

GREAT BRITISH PUB DOGS

5 *Mr Jones*

FISHERMAN'S ARMS, PLYMOUTH

'Mr Jones has his own beer, a premium golden bitter, pale and hoppy at 4.5 per cent.'

Name Mr Jones

Breed Miniature schnauzer

Age Four

Owner Donna Phillips and Lee Chambers

Mr Jones in three words Lovable, shy, adventurous.

Favourite spot On his 'reserved for the dog' cushions, and by the window.

Key fact He has his own beer, a premium golden bitter, pale and hoppy at 4.5 per cent. Mr Jones chooses not to partake, though.

Loves Going for walks. He's highly excitable in the mornings at the prospect of going outside. He also prefers dogs to humans.

Best doggy friend Itsy, a black lab. They hare around the pub together and tug over toys.

Purpose in the pub Meeter and greeter – especially the dogs (and most especially the female ones).

6 Flora

THE NESS, TEIGNMOUTH, DEVON

Name Flora

Breed Cockapoo

Age in photo Three months

Owners Tom and Emma Hunt. Tom originally went to look at her brother but chose Flora instead, after she got hiccups from being so excited. At the time Flora could fit in a beanie hat.

Flora in three words Sociable, lunatic, cute.

Locals' favourite There are several regulars at the pub who take Flora out for walks, including an elderly lady whose dog has died and who doesn't want a new one.

Favourite place to walk On the beach, anywhere along the coast, Torquay, Haldon forest.

Loves Frolicking on the beach. Eating sand until she's sick. Chasing birds. All people.

Hates Water, although if she's playing with other dogs by the sea she will copy them and jump in.

Best doggy friend Storm, a collie – they're crazy for each other. Storm's owner lives in the café up the road. She and the family cat, Hooch, make a good team too.

Pub nugget It was an officer's mess during world war two, and was built in 1810 by the same man who built the smuggler's tunnel that runs behind the pub.

'They're inseparable, like sisters.'

Name Honey

Breed Saluki

Age Ten

Owner Alison Weaver

Back story Both dogs were saved from sorry circumstances. Honey was being kept in an allotment shed in Newcastle and was very sick when Alison collected her.

Honey in three words Hardy, elegant, quiet.

Loves Being petted, chasing squirrels, and running. She'll run the whole perimeter of the nearby downs and barely break sweat.

Hates Tight spaces, due to being partially blind.

Dynamic Honey is the boss inside the pub. Outside, Dolly often comes to her aid. Other dogs are fascinated by Honey, who gets unnerved by the attention. She puts out a distress call and Dolly comes running in and saves Honey by bashing them aside with her shoulder.

In the wars Honey was once knocked down by a van, leaving her with a punctured lung, two broken ribs and a 'head like a melon'. She is now blind in one eye, so she falls over if she runs around a tight corner, and won't jump over anything. She was also attacked by an Alsatian and got a dislocated leg.

Name Dolly (aka 'the D-Dog')

Breed Staffy/greyhound cross

Age Ten

Back story Dolly's owners moved to Saudi Arabia and left her in the house with a big bag of food and a bucket of water. A neighbour heard her crying and broke in. Alison got her and Honey on the same day, and they've been inseparable ever since.

Dolly in three words Protective, presence, sociable.

Loves Wandering around socialising, and the cool leather sofas when it's warm.

Hates Other dogs scaring Honey.

Dolly the community dog She often wanders out to the Port of Call pub next door (also owned by Alison), or the Coach and Horses down the road (which isn't). She also goes to the nearby fish shop and watches people eating. Both dogs get recognised a lot locally.

8 Hetty

QUAYSIDE, WHITSTABLE, KENT

Name Hetty

Breed King Charles spaniel

Age Eighteen months

Owner Emma Collins, Stuart Curtis, and daughters Matilda and Nell

Behind the name She was named after the Quayside's previous dog, Henry. 'My daughters originally called her Henrietta, but we've managed to get it down to Hettie,' says Emma.

Hetty in three words Cuddly, sweet, hoover.

Likes Sitting in the pub window, sleeping under the duvet.

Dislikes Rain, dog food.

Purpose in the pub Hostess. She'll say hello to anyone, so long as they have a nice comfy lap. She's the world's worst guard dog though – she completely ignores the burglar alarm.

Best friends Maggie the French bulldog, and Jess the Jack Russell from the nearby pet shop.

Special move Actually cuddling. First the paws go on your shoulders, then she presses herself into you.

9 *Betty*

NEW INN, WHITSTABLE, KENT

Name Betty (Kennel Club name is Beretta Storm).

Breed Labrador retriever

Age Three

Owners Becka and Roy McKay

Behind the name She is named after Bet Lynch from *Coronation Street*.

Betty in three words Loving, greedy and shy (at first).

Loves Playing fetch with her ball, swimming in the sea, playing with their cat, Peggy.

Hates Being left alone.

Pub dog technique She only interacts with the ones she likes. If you're one of her favourites she'll bestow plenty of cuddles and licks.

Odd habit She hides Roy's hats under her bed. Also, after her night-time toilet she runs around like a loon, spinning in circles.

Best friend There are lots of dog friends – Molly, Coco, Sasha, Jarvis, Zeus – but she's extra protective of Peggy the cat, keeping dogs away from her.

Pub nugget It used to be called the Bricklayers Arms, and was the first purpose-built pub in town for the old 'Crab and Winkle' railway line between Whitstable and Canterbury.

'Hachi is an extreme sports dog – rock climbing, cliff jumping and swimming into coastal caves.'

Name Hachi, short for Hachiko

Breed Staffordshire bull terrier

Age in photos Nearly five

Owner Toby Slade

Named after The famous Japanese film star dog from the 1920s/30s.

Hachi in three words Loving, demanding, mischievous.

Best doggy friend Yoshi, a bull terrier/ Staffy cross.

Favourite spot in the pub Anywhere she can get attention.

Favourite game Tug-of-war.

Unusual hobby Hachi is an extreme sports dog. She has joined owner Toby for 'coasteering' expeditions in Devon – rock climbing, cliff jumping and swimming into coastal caves.

11 Beth

BLACK DOG, WHITSTABLE, KENT

PUB DOG
CAPITAL OF
BRITAIN

Name Beth

Breed Border collie

Age Three

Owners Mike and Carmel McWilliam

Beth in three words Friendly, athletic, greedy.

Loves Running, and running, and running. She is Carmel's running buddy, and twice a week they do 10km+ together around nearby Seasalter.

Hates Very big dogs and fireworks.

Favourite spot in the pub None, she's too sociable to stay still and works her way around the tables.

Eats Anything except spinach.

Favourite regular John, who sits by the big bowl of dog treats. In fact, anyone who sits by the big bowl of dog treats.

Why have a resident dog in a pub 'In a way it adds a human touch, as dogs are man's best friend. So people feel at home when they come in and see a dog, especially one who's so welcoming.'

Best friends The ragbag pack of dogs she goes running with on Whitstable beach.

Scare story She once escaped over a fence and on to the beach when she was a puppy. She had a whole crowd of people chasing after her.

'Loves running, and running, and running. She is Carmel's running buddy, and twice a week they do 10km+ ...'

12 Barney

SMACK INN, WHITSTABLE, KENT

Name Barney

Breed Working cocker spaniel

Age Five

Owners Tiffany Kirtikar and Mark Flood

Favourite spot In front of the fire, or in a quiet corner with a customer.

Barney's double life Away from the pub, he lives on Mark's ninety-acre farm with two Labradors, Molly and Ben. At the farm he tears around and gets harassed by the chickens. In the pub, he curls up like a granddad in the corner.

Favourite place to walk Whitstable beach.

Loves Being showered with attention by kids (for a little while, then he stoically tolerates it).

Doesn't like Small dogs, loud banging (Barney is not an in-demand gun dog).

Best dog friend Ruby the mongrel is his best friend, also Boris the Staffy, and Hetty the spaniel from the Quayside.

Distinctive mark He has a bald patch on his tail from wagging it against things.

Pub nugget Before it became the Smack Inn, the property was owned by the captain of one of the local oyster dredgers (Whitstable being famed for its oysters). It's said he opened it up as a 'bottle and jug' (i.e. an unoffical pub), before it became a pub. A 'smack' is an oyster dredger boat.

13 *Rita*

EAST KENT HOTEL, WHITSTABLE, KENT

PUB DOG
CAPITAL OF
BRITAIN

Name Rita

Breed English bulldog

Age Two

Owners Spix, Dotty and Ruby Outram

Behind the name Spix named her after Corry legend Rita Fairclough.

Rita in three words Playful, beautiful, fat.

Favourite spot in the pub By the cold air vent from the fridges.

Loves Water (Rita likes lying in puddles), getting cuddles from patrons, and playing (word to the wise: if you give her a little attention you are contractually obliged to play for a bit).

Hates Cushions. If you hold a cushion towards her, she will back off rapidly looking sorrowful.

Best dog friend Henry the spaniel, who Rita has played with in the garden for hours.

Special move Leaping and jumping and spinning like a ballerina when she's excited and senses that play is afoot.

'Playful, beautiful, fat...'

14 *Gizmo*
LONDON TAVERN, MARGATE, KENT

'Danny la Rue apparently used to sleep
in the pub cellar when he was playing at the
Theatre Royal down the road.'

Name Gizmo

Breed Lhasa apso

Age He turned seventeen in April

Owners Nancy and Carl Bradley

Gizmo in three words Stubborn,
independent, sociable.

Favourite spot In his bed by the fire in the
pub.

Loves Going for car rides, being with
people.

Hates People riding bikes.

Best doggy friend Louis, another Lhasa
apso who belongs to owner Nancy's sister.

Odd habit Sometimes at around midnight
he'll run around like a loon – but if you
say 'freeze' and clap your hands, he stops
immediately.

Bad habit 'Gizzy' has a tendency to wander
off to Hawley Square opposite, where he
has on occasion been found loitering late
at night.

Pub nuggets Danny la Rue apparently
used to sleep in the pub cellar when he
was playing at the Theatre Royal down the
road. There is a system of three tunnels
underneath the pub: one an actor's passage
leading straight to the theatre (*see* La Rue),
one to Hawley Square, and a smuggler's
tunnel that goes to Fort Hill on the coast.
Gizmo is too scared to go down into the
cellar.

Name Dave

Breed Irish wolfhound

Age Three

Owners Ken and Fiona Shewring

Dave in three words Crazy, fast, lovable.

Height Just under 7ft on his back legs.

Weight 101kg (16 stone).

Favourite spot Right in the centre of the bar, in everybody's way.

Best doggy friend Koda, a Japanese akita. They chase each other round the pub, share treats, go for walks, then sleep together.

Favourite food Roast dinner. Any roast – Dave doesn't care.

Favourite drink A cup of tea first thing in the morning.

Loves Chasing the trains down by the railway crossing, and playing with the swans by the River Stour.

Hates Small dogs who yap. Dave sticks his nose up and walks away.

Lest we forget Derek, Dave's brother who died in March 2016 on his third birthday.

Pub dog technique He lies on the floor and wraps his leg around a customer's leg until they give him some attention.

Pub nuggets The pub dates back to 1547 as a former coaching inn.

16 *Bruno*

ZETLAND ARMS, KINGSDOWN, KENT

Name Bruno

Breed Black Labrador

Time at the pub 2012–16, he died aged twelve and a half

Owners Kerensa and Tom Miller

Bruno in three words Laid-back, friendly, loyal.

Loves Food, food, food. Preferably anything meaty.

How did he work it off? Swimming in the sea, attending BBQs on the beach, and playing football in the garden.

Hated Being picked up.

Best doggy friends No particular individual but Bruno loved small dogs, especially spaniels and the occasional Chihuahua.

Favourite spot On the floor between the bar and the cutlery drawer. That's where customers would find him for some petting.

Favourite customer Lav. They went on fishing trips together.

17 Loki

THE RUMSEY WELLS, NORWICH

Name Loki

Breed Alaskan malamute

Age Two

Owner Steve Bishop-Laggett

The story behind the name He was going to be called Murdoch, after Howling Mad Murdoch from the *A-Team*, as he spent his first night at Steve's flat howling constantly. Shortly after, Loki wrecked the sofa (for the first time) and most of the carpet, so Steve renamed him 'Loki', as it means 'god of mischief'.

Loki in three words Fearless, diva, hyperactive.

Likes Hoarding meat around Steve's flat. Digging holes in Steve's sofa. Ripping up Steve's carpet. Doing whatever Steve is doing.

Doesn't like Being on his lead. Alarms and sirens (they only bring more howling).

The running dog Loki can run, and run, and run. For long distances and without stopping – as Steve found out when Loki once escaped. A forty-five-minute cat-and-mouse ensued around Norwich city centre.

Food Loki loves 'really disgusting food' according to Steve, i.e. chicken carcasses, hearts, offal, and racks of ribs – and he prefers frozen to fresh.

Drink He doesn't drink much water, as his breed is used to running for miles without stopping for rehydration. He is partial to an Adnam's pale ale, though.

Best doggy friend Olly, a golden retriever.

The god of mischief After a particularly productive sofa-destroying session, Loki tried to get away with it by attempting to push the incoming Steve away from the room where it had occurred. He then lay on his back with a soppy face, refusing to look at what remained of the sofa while Steve pointed at it.

Pub nugget The pub is part of a stretch of premises that used to be the renowned hatmakers, Herbert Rumsey Wells. There are several nods in the pub towards its hat-making past.

'Zuri means "beautiful" in Swahili.'

Name Zuri

Breed Rhodesian ridgeback

Age Five

Owner Lorna Bevan-Thompson

Why is she called Zuri? It means 'beautiful' in Swahili.

Zuri in three words Quirky, loyal, faithful.

Loves Wandering freely around the pub, being in the sunshine, playing with other dogs on the beach.

Hates The rain. She runs away from it. Also, Lorna's pet black-headed macaque called Pidge, who sometimes makes a guest appearance down in the pub.

Best doggy friend There are several contenders but it has to be Gizmo (a terrier/Lhasa apso cross), who is Lorna's niece's dog, and Lila, her mum's shih-tzu.

Pub nugget The Lacon Arms won 'the UK's most dog-friendly pub' in 2015.

19 Ollie

PLOUGH INN, WANGFORD, SUFFOLK

Name Ollie. His pedigree name is Lancelot the Great

Breed Dogue de Bordeaux

Age Six

Owner Tony Vile

Weight 68kg (10 stone).

Where from The Dogue de Bordeaux Rehome and Rescue Society. Ollie was rescued at the age of eighteen months from a flat in Liverpool.

Ollie in three words Nothing fazes him.

Loves Running in the fields and down by the sea at Southwold beach. Also, mixing with other dogs, so long as they're not intimidated by his size.

Hates Little dogs. He's scared of them, and often hides if one comes in the pub.

Purpose in the pub To be laid-back with customers, and a good deterrent at night.

Pub dog technique He normally approaches regulars with a wagging tail in the hope of some attention.

ANGEL INN, WANGFORD, SUFFOLK

MOST
PRESENTABLE
AWARD

'Her mum, Mayfair Margarita,
won "junior bitch" at the 2013 Crufts.'

Name Malibu Heartthrob, or 'Boo'

Breed Standard poodle

Age Three

Owners Peter and Christine White

Behind the name All their animals have been partially named after alcohol, and her dad had Coconut in his name, so it had to be Malibu.

Boo in three words Gregarious, dignified, pretty.

Purpose in the pub To be head of security, though few people take her seriously in this role. She only got the promotion after Crème de Cacao died in Christmas 2015.

Loves Sprinting and being patted. She has the impression the world was put there to pat her.

Hates Not much – but enter the pub when it's empty and she'll growl at you a bit.

Pedigree pooch Her mum, Mayfair Margarita, won 'junior bitch' at the 2013 Crufts. Two others from the same litter were grand champions in Australia.

Favourite spot Exactly where her grandma, Crème de Cacao, used to sit: in front of the bar facing the door.

Key quote 'Boo is a huge part of the pub and our time here. It wouldn't be the same without her.'

GREAT BRITISH PUB DOGS

21 *Dilly*

STAR INN, WENHASTON, SUFFOLK

Name Dilly

Breed Bearded collie/lurcher cross

Age Nine and a half

Owners Carl and Virginia Ernsting

Behind the name He was christened by the Dogs Trust who rescued him from a life wandering the streets of Dublin.

Dilly in three words Confident, soft, beautiful.

Loves Going off with Toby (see Best friend) for hours on end, digging in the bushes. They come back covered in earth.

Hates Bright lights, and being groomed with anything metal.

Favourite food Any meat, especially roast chicken.

Favourite toy He has lots of toys but the ones he likes he rips apart.

Favourite spot in the bar At the bar hatch, where he can see and smell everything.

Best friend Toby, a Jack Russell. He used to live opposite the pub but moved away to East Bergholt. It's OK, though, Toby comes round for sleepovers.

Walking spot The common at Wenhaston. Further afield, he loves the forest at Dunwich, the beach at Sizewell, and Dorset where he holidays each year.

Around the pub He approaches the locals who bring him in biscuits or dish out the cuddles.

Unusual habit Barking at the moon and streetlights, possibly because they were always present when he was a stray.

22 *Franco*

QUEEN'S HEAD, EYE, SUFFOLK

Name Franco

Breed Rottweiler/black Labrador cross

Age Two

Owner Leigh Gardiner

Behind the name He is named after the Chelsea legend Gianfranco Zola.

Franco in three words Loving, boisterous, loyal.

Loves Eating. He once ate 5kg of gammon that he found. Always up for a pork scratching.

Favourite toys Tennis balls, rope, and people.

Best friend Ziggy, a husky/German shepherd cross whom he loves dearly.

Pub dog technique Franco is in the pub all day, so he mills about with customers all the time, pawing them for attention or putting a ball down to get them to play with him. Guest dog walkers often come and take him out – he's a local celebrity.

Favourite walking spot The moors, where he meets up with his pals.

Purpose in the pub Pub mascot and friend to everyone who comes in. People always ask if they can't see him.

Scare story He went missing once when he decided to leave the pub for a day outing with Chunk from next door.

MOST
PUB DOGGY
PUB

'They provide comfort, get people talking and are an asset to our community pub ...'

GREAT BRITISH PUB DOGS

Names Bonnie and Miss Havisham ('Havi')

Breeds They are both miniature dachshunds; Bonnie a long-haired and Miss Havisham a long-hair/wire-hair cross

Ages Bonnie is three, Havi is five.

Owner Laura King

Bonnie and Havi in three words Bonnie – loud, licky, lovable. Havi – affectionate, intelligent, bossy.

Favourite food/drink Havi would gladly spend her day licking drips of beer off the floor. Bonnie likes anything she can obtain covertly.

Favourite toys Havi likes to hoard soft toys in her bed, Bonnie is a sucker for tennis balls.

What are they like to handle? Havi will not let you stop petting her, she'll lick you or prod you with her nose until you submit. Bonnie will sit on your knee all day if you let her.

Doggy friend/nemesis The pub is extremely popular with dog owners, so they have lots of friends, but Bonnie does have a pub dog nemesis – Noodles, a poodle cross at another nearby pub. Bonnie can't walk past the pub without losing the plot. If they accidentally cross paths they become a blurred ball of angry fluff. Havi will be friends with anyone as long as they don't try to sniff her bum.

Purpose around the pub 'We shouldn't underestimate the healing power of pooches: "The sausages", as they're affectionately known, know when you need their unconditional love. They provide comfort, bring people together, get people talking and are an asset to our community pub.'

24 Dolly

DEAD CRAFTY BEER COMPANY, LIVERPOOL

'Even though it's a city centre pub it's a real local's pub, for the community. Having a dog in the bar just adds to that.'

Name Dolly

Breed Tibetan terrier

Age Four

Owners Vicky and Gareth Morgan

The story behind the name After Vicky and Gareth put their name down to take the unnamed dog, they went on holiday to the USA and visited Dollywood, Dolly Parton's theme park in Tennessee. And the name was born . . .

Dolly in three words Scruffy, playful, nervous.

Favourite food All cheese. Dolly is allergic to all meat.

Loves Rolling around on her back, pottering around in the garden and the allotment, sitting by the fire at home.

Hates Surprise noises. As a nervous dog she is easily spooked.

Her role in the pub Bouncer. She checks out everyone who comes in.

Unusual habit Sleeping on her back with her legs in the air.

Why have a pub dog? 'Even though it's a city centre pub it's a real local's pub, for the community. Having a dog in the bar just adds to that.'

Pub nuggets The pub only opened in 2016. The premises were previously closed for twelve years, and before that were a typewriter repair shop and tobacconist. As a beer specialist the pub has twenty different keg beers at any time.

Name Jura

Breed Bull mastiff

Age Three

Owners Stephanie Price and Craig Frame

Jura in three words Big, slobbery softy.

A day in the life Sleep, eat, sleep, bark, sleep, repeat.

Loves Any food, from celery to horse poo to goose. One exception: canned shrimp.

Hates The hoover. She's also not a fan of the kitchen, but it's a love/hate relationship as that's where the food is.

How does she interact with the locals? She gives them the sad puppy-dog eyes to try and get her paws on their crisps (even though she's never allowed them). Sometimes she finds a new family and just sits with them for the afternoon.

Does she have a favourite regular? Elaine, her main celery provider. Jura absolutely loves celery.

Pub nugget Gullivers has a music venue, hosting touring bands from all over the world – many of which Jura loves to bark along with.

Name Matilda

Breed Yorkiepoo

Age About ten weeks in photos

Owner Simon Crompton

Matilda in three words Giddypants, loving, non-stop.

Favourite spot In her bed bought by one of the customers. It was in the far corner where it was less busy, but she was too nosy to stay there, so the bed was moved.

Loves Chewing anything, and fetching. She also loves underwear – hiding it, putting it on herself, going through it in the washing basket . . . Simon has to stash his underwear in a high place.

Pub dog technique She says hello to everybody and receives a lot of attention. Lots of customers come in requesting to take her for a walk.

Scare story Matilda disappeared from Simon's house, escaping via the back yard. Luckily she turned up at his other pub, The Healey.

Pub nugget It's a multi-award-winning pub, bagging the CAMRA National Pub of the Year in 2012, and Manchester Pub of the Year on three occasions.

'Lots of customers come in requesting to take her for a walk ...'

27 *Bam Bam*

THE FREEMASONS, WISWELL, CLITHEROE, LANCASHIRE

GREAT BRITISH PUB DOGS

Name Bam Bam

Breed Bulldog

Age Two

Owner Steven Smith

The story behind the name Steven admits he's not the best at helping with housework, so his partner, Aga, used to say they were like the Flintstones, living in the Stone Age. They named Bam Bam to keep with the theme.

Bam Bam in three words Energetic, lovable, charming.

Favourite food Scrambled eggs and ham, and the pub roast beef on a Sunday. He also likes a little Guinness.

Favourite toys An antler, seems to keep him happy for hours. He also goes wild for a tissue.

Favourite spot In the Chesterfield armchair. He looks very regal in it.

Best doggy friend Otto, a Hungarian vizsla who lives in the village.

Pub nugget It's been named the No.1 pub by the *Good Food Guide* for the past three years, and is the only pub to receive the coveted 7/10 score.

'His favourite food is scrambled eggs and ham, and the pub roast beef on a Sunday.'

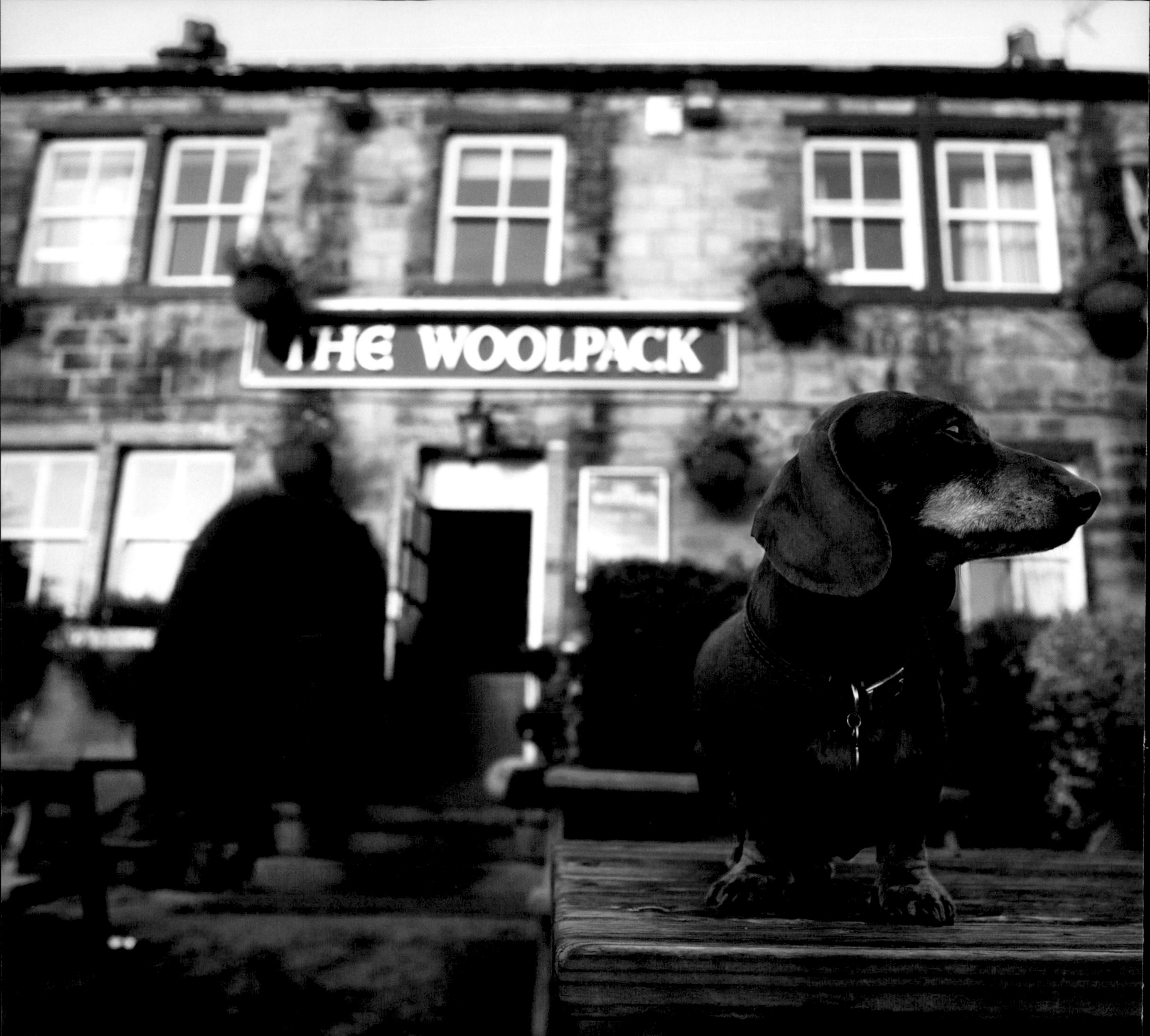
HE WOOLPACK

28 *Frank*

THE WOOLPACK, ESHOLT, WEST YORKSHIRE

'The Yorkshire Dachshund Club meets at the pub several times a year, thirty dachshunds turn up, and Frank leads the walk.'

Name Frank

Breed Short-haired miniature dachshund

Age Eight

Owner James Downey

Why call him Frank? It's a big, strong English name.

Frank in three words Little old man.

Favourite place to walk Up in Esholt woods.

Favourite spot in the pub Next to the fire.

Loves Chasing a ball, relaxing, and his fluffy toy which is his comfort blanket.

Hates The rain and snow, and being left in the house alone (he will use his nose to bang the letter box to get your attention).

Role in the pub He's the pub mascot. The Yorkshire Dachshund Club meets at the pub several times a year, thirty dachshunds turn up, and Frank leads the walk.

Key fact A few years ago three discs exploded in his spine. James was told Frank would never walk again. They had to teach him to walk with only his front legs by lifting up his back legs with a scarf and walking him around as if he was a wheelbarrow. They tried hydrotherapy too, and on the very day they got the keys to the pub in 2015, Frank walked on his back legs again for the first time. They all promptly burst into tears. As a tribute to Frank's hardiness, James got a huge tattoo in a particularly painful spot – from his hip up to his armpit.

Pub nugget It is best known for being the local pub in *Emmerdale* for over twenty years. The most recent filming took place in the pub in late 2016.

'Her name comes from one of pub's popular cask beers, Copper Dragon Golden Pippin.'

Name Pippin

Breed Collie cross

Age Three and a half

Owners Tom and Robbie Kitt

Behind the name The name comes from one of the pub's popular cask beers, Copper Dragon Golden Pippin.

Pippin in three words Intelligent, friendly, fun.

Loves Obliterating soft toys, playing with beer mats, long walks, the butcher.

Hates Water and the postman.

Favourite spot In her chair, or lazing in the front lounge window getting her photo taken by tourists.

Best friend Delsa, a black lab, and her love interest is Marley a German shepherd/husky although he's too old for her.

Walking spots Her daily walk is around York Minster and the city walls. Her longer walks include Clifton Ings riverbank and trips to the seaside.

Purpose in the pub To listen – she always hears the doorbell and deliveries before Tom and Robbie do.

Interaction with the locals Pippin is a highly popular dog – the customers' favourite amusement is to throw beer mats for her to chase, although she hasn't got the hang of picking them up.

Name Shot (Kennel Club name is Roughbeat Balthazarr)

Breed Golden retriever

Age Two

Owners Paul and Carol Forster

The story behind the name Paul and Carol held a competition in the pub to name their new puppy at £1 per go, the proceeds of which went to the Golden Retriever Rescue Society. They chose the name 'Shot' after his uncle, who was a champion gun dog from Essex.

Shot in three words Friendly, playful, curious.

Walking spots Down by the 'Rivers Meet' where the North Tyne meets the South Tyne. Many locals ask to take him out.

Pub dog technique Shot welcomes everybody and loves being fussed over. He plays with children, inviting them over to his toy box. He carries his lead to anybody who will take him for a walk – especially George Stoker who takes him out regularly, and his auntie Ailsa and uncle Robin who spoil him.

Favourite spot Down by Jackie's feet on a Sunday. She's one of the locals and he sits beneath her where it's hard to be spotted, awaiting bar snacks.

Best friend Boo, one local's chocolate lab who is two days younger. Then all the staff who constantly play with him.

Pub dog dynasty Shot had big shoes to fill as he took the reins from another retriever called Levi, who died in 2014 and was virtually a local celebrity, but 'Shot has made such an impact we know he'll never be forgotten either.'

GREAT BRITISH PUB DOGS

GREAT BRITISH PUB DOGS

Name Simba

Breed Weimaraner

Age Nine

Owner Caroline Saul

His back story Simba was in a house in Alnwick that was raided by the police. Caroline was part of the raid as an antisocial behaviour officer. Inside they found dozens of dogs living in appalling conditions, including Simba who was sitting in the corner, sick and extremely thin. He was seventeen months old at the time. Caroline fostered him through the RSPCA with the intention of someone else adopting him, but then couldn't bring herself to give him away.

Simba in three words Committed, fun, loving.

Favourite food/drink Haggis and egg, and cappuccino.

Favourite toys His soft panda and tennis balls.

Favourite spot Beside the fire.

Closest companion Poppy, a cockador – it's true love.

Any unusual habits He used to be able to pickpocket people's purses.

Tilly and River

BUCK INN, CHOP GATE, NORTH YORK MOORS

Names Tilly and River

Breed Giant schnauzers

Ages Tilly is five, River is six.

Owners Wolfgang and Helen Barth

Three words to describe them River –
laid-back, outdoorsy, active. Tilly – playful,
competitive, homely.

Back story River was 'saved from a life as
a show dog' – he was shown and won a
couple of prizes, but injured his tail.

Best friend Mack, a local border collie.
They play in the garden together, and
cuddle up and sleep together.

Favourite walking spot In the forest at Clay
Bank Top, where they can run free. On the
moors they have to be on a lead.

Likes Tilly loves playing in the garden,
River loves big walks.

Dislikes They don't like dog food, they
prefer real meat, carrots and apples.

Favourite toys Tilly loves her balls, River
has a little stuffed puppy – it's the only
thing he hasn't destroyed.

33 Frank

BRANDLING VILLA, NEWCASTLE

Name Frank

Breed 'Economy beagle', ie half-beagle, half-Jack Russell

Age Ten

Owner Dave Carr

Bought from A rather questionable man in County Durham. He tried to sell Dave a ferret on the way out.

Behind the name Frank's Sunday name is actually Franco, after Francis Begbie from *Trainspotting*. This was so Dave could shout 'Nice one Franco!' if he went to the toilet somewhere he shouldn't.

Favourite food/drink Bin meat, carrots, and chicken sticks from Sainsbury's. His favourite beer is Theakston's Old Peculier.

Favourite toy He loves a sock.

Any strange habits, good or bad? Frank likes to sit in on meetings, but he ruins the pub's Trip Advisor rating with his incessant scrounging.

Favourite spot At his table in the window.

Interaction with the locals Everyone loves Frank. The regulars bring in treats for him.

Best friend Fellow pub dog Winston, from the Black Bull in Morpeth.

Nemesis Craig David, The Free Trade Inn's cat.

Scary moment When he fell through the ice in a local pond. The fire brigade came, and surprise surprise, they all knew him.

The joy of having a pub dog 'It's hard to be the "community landlord" now, as the job is so demanding and multi-faceted. Frank can play host in my absence. He's also pleased to see people all the time, even when my lust for hospitality suffers.'

Claim to fame He's been in newspapers in India, Detroit, Japan, Estonia, Chile, China, Russia . . . and in the *Daily Mail*.

Susie, Molly, Bella

TAN HILL INN, SWALEDALE, YORKSHIRE DALES

'It's the most unique pub I've come across,' says Louise,
'you get smelly walkers, lord of the manor – everyone,
all at the same time.'

Name Bella

Breed Maremma (Italian sheepdog)

Age Five

Owners Vanessa and Nigel Graham
(bar managers)

Bella in three words Trustworthy, loyal,
scaredy-cat.

Loves Running free and chasing rabbits.
Also partial to a drop of red wine.

Hates Bella is scared of 'almost everything'.

Name Susie

Breed Working cocker

Age Four

Owners Louise and Mike Peace
(pub owners)

Pub dog dynasty Susie was a gift to the
Peaces from a customer, who saw how
upset they were about losing their springer
spaniel, Izzy. Louise returned the favour to
the customer last year. Prior to Izzy there
was Sherbert, a wire-haired dachshund,
and Ollie, a shih tzu who they got on
the day they moved into the pub. Jara,
a German shepherd joined the team in
early 2017.

Susie in three words Intelligent, snob,
loyal.

Loves Stealing Louise's shoes and taking
them to her bed. No one else's, just Louise's

Pub dog technique It's a sort of 'stroke me
if you have to'.

Scaredy-dogs refuge The pub has hosted
anti-fireworks nights, where owners can
bring their dogs for a blissfully stress-free
5th November.

Name Molly

Breed Drakeshead Labrador

Age Three

Owners Louise and Mike Peace
(pub owners)

Molly in three words Clumsy, needy, hungry.

Loves Molly and Susie both love swimming in the brook near the pub. When they go in the sea they dive down and retrieve bones from the bottom.

Hates When Louise shouts at them.

Pub dog technique Molly runs up to every customer who enters, wagging her tail and barking. Some people misconstrue the barking as aggression but it's really just a loud, enthusiastic welcome.

Why have resident dogs? 'You get a different clientele. The people in the pub are more likely to be warm and down-to-earth, not uptight about a dog wandering about. If someone doesn't like dogs then I'm happy to pull them away, but if someone asks why they're there, I say if you don't like it, piss off.'

Pub nugget #1 The Tan Hill is the highest pub in the UK at 528 metres above sea level – it's so remote it's off the National Grid.

Pub nugget #2 In the eighteenth century it served the local mine workers. The last nearby mine closed in 1929 and the miners' cottages were demolished soon after, but the pub remained.

Pub nugget #3 The pub and its surroundings have had numerous TV/film shoots and celebrity visits. These include: *Robin Hood Prince of Thieves*, *Harry Potter*, Kyle MacLachlan (*Twin Peaks*) for a Vodafone ad, an episode of *Top Gear*, *All Creatures Great and Small*, and *The Fast Show*. Mark Little (Joe Mangel from *Neighbours*) and Griff Rhys Jones are among the celebs who have drunk there.

Pub nugget #4 It has hosted gigs, with visiting bands including Arctic Monkeys, British Sea Power and Mark Ronson.

Janet and Douglas

BODA BAR, EDINBURGH

Names Janet and Douglas

Breed Boston terriers

Ages Janet is two and a half, Douglas is one.

Owner Ella Hopps

Behind their names Ella and her partner have a strong dislike for dog names, so they went for more human names. Douglas was very nearly called Steven.

Janet and Douglas in three words Janet – intelligent, aware, loving. Douglas – hilarious, daft, energetic.

Favourite toys Janet has one ball to shred and another to chase, over and over and over again.

Douglas loves a tea towel, which he steals out of Ella's pocket when she's working.

Favourite spot Janet – someone's lap, by the window or in the big armchair. Douglas – his bed behind the bar.

Best friend Janet prefers humans inside the pub, but races around with dogs outside. Douglas's best friend is Janet, whether she likes it or not. He also has a best whippet pal called Kanga.

Purpose in the pub To entertain Ella and the customers with their nonsense.

Scare story Janet once got run over, but luckily she was a tiny puppy and emerged from between the wheels remarkably unscathed.

Brush with fame Janet made friends with Alan Cumming in Sofi's bar, (the sister bar nearby) during the 2016 Edinburgh Fringe. She made sure he knew who she was, and persistently sat on his lap.

Pub nugget The bar is named after a small hamlet in Sweden with only ten inhabitants, where one of the owners grew up.

GREAT BRITISH PUB DOGS

'He's bilingual. He was trained in French when he was young. So when he's in trouble, Ash speaks to him in French so he knows he's being told off …'

Name Hero

Breed English bulldog

Age Five

Owner Ash Bibby

Behind the name Ash was living in France when she got him. The pedigree rules in France meant his name had to begin with 'H'. Also it looks like he has a hero mask on, and an eyepatch, and as Ash puts it 'he turned into my hero'.

Ash in three words My whole world. 'I've dedicated my pub to him – all over Edinburgh people recognise Hero and know the pub because of him.'

Loves Spherical objects. He used to destroy footballs until he realised they're more fun undestroyed. Loves balloons, and can sniff out a tennis ball from behind anything. Ash filled the pub with soft play balls for his birthday, and he tried to crush them all.

Hates Being left behind anywhere. He wants to be where Ash is.

Best doggy mate There are many . . . Abel the pug, Bear the Boston terrier who belongs to barmaid Ellie, Stella the three-legged Jack Russell.

Special move He's bilingual. He was trained in French when he was young. So when he's in trouble, Ash speaks to him in French so he knows he's being told off like he's a puppy again.

Scare story He once disappeared when they were out in town – he had walked himself back to the pub, trotting across roads by himself.

Why have a dog in a pub? 'It makes it so much more homely and relatable. Dogs can sense feelings, when people are sad or happy, they're really good at giving people what they need. It makes the pub a home away from home for a lot of people who are on their own, or want a dog but can't have one for whatever reason.'

37 *Akila*

SHERIFFMUIR INN, DUNBLANE, STIRLING, CENTRAL SCOTLAND

Name Akila

Breed Irish soft-coated wheaten terrier

Age Three

Owners Moira and Geoff Cook

Time at the pub 2014–2017. Sadly Akila and the Cooks left the Sheriffmuir Inn in January 2017, and Akila died shortly afterwards.

Behind the name Akila is a Swahili girl's name. The name came to the Cooks during a trip to Edinburgh Zoo. They walked around the zoo calling out the name to see if it sounded strange – and it stuck.

In three words Enthusiastic, fun, loving.

Favourite spot Down by Moira's feet in reception.

Loved Playing with Moira and Geoff's close friends and family.

Hated The window cleaner.

Pub nugget #1 The Sheriffmuir Inn dates back to the late seventeenth century, and overlooks the site of the 1715 Battle of Sheriffmuir during the Jacobite rising.

Pub nugget #2 The pub was famous for being home to Hercules, an 8ft, 70-stone pet grizzly bear. Andy Robin – a wrestler – and his wife Maggie adopted him and he became Andy's wrestling partner, making

hundreds of appearances on the UK circuit. He starred in many films, TV shows and adverts, most notably in *Octopussy* alongside Roger Moore. In the pub, Andy would bring Hercules down among the locals and feed him beer and cherries, and practise wrestling moves with him in the fields outside. Remarkably he never attacked any people or livestock.

38 *Biscuit*

STEAM PACKET INN, ISLE OF WHITHORN, DUMFRIES AND GALLOWAY

'Biscuit hates baths (he looks like a rat when he's wet).'

Name Biscuit

Breed Micro Pomeranian

Age Three

Owner Alastair Scoular

Biscuit in three words Loyal, furball, cute (and he knows it).

Loves Attention, chasing roe deer – he thinks he's a cross between a deerhound and a spaniel. He thinks it's hilarious when the deer run away.

Hates Thinking he's being left behind. He gets anxious when he sees bags by the door and thinks he's being left. Also, baths (he looks like a rat when he's wet).

Eats Pepperoni and chorizo.

Best friend Alastair's spaniel puppy, Coco.

Favourite spot in the bar Under Alastair's stool.

Pub nugget The Steam Packet Inn has been in the family for forty years, has won numerous CAMRA awards, and was named *Countryfile* rural pub of the year 2016.

39 *Rolo*

'He loves anything that squeaks, then destroying it until it squeaks no more.'

Name Rolo

Breed Boxer

Age Four

Owner Damian Devine

Food A very specific and regimented hypoallergenic diet, because of a dietary problem. He has the occasional beef bone which can make him very flatulent.

Favourite walking spots Barnard Park, Clissold Park, Regent's Canal and sometimes Victoria Park.

The story behind the name Damian had a boxer called Rolo at the pub for ten years, until she died in 2012. In 2013 a friend tipped him off that a rescue centre in Bishop's Stortford had a boxer called Rolo, so he went to visit and couldn't resist taking him. Rolo mk II is named after the perfect white 'r' shape on his head.

Rolo in three words Very laid-back.

Favourite spot In his basket in the bar, or by the window, watching the city workers and college students walk by.

Unusual habit Weeing on dumped Christmas trees, and sleeping upside down with his head hanging off the edge of the chair.

Loves Anything that squeaks, then destroying it until it squeaks no more.

Hates High-vis jackets.

Why have a pub dog? 'In a city pub the people who come here can't have pets or grew up with a dog, so they come in and it's a sort of pet therapy. They're also rarer now as pubs are more sterile and run by chains and worried about health and safety.'

Pub history

★ The Old Red Lion might be the oldest pub in London. It's said to date back to 1415 and Damian has traced it officially back to 1500.

★ One of William Hogarth's lithographs features the pub in the background, with Sadler's Wells in the foreground. A local journalist in 1947 entered the pub to find two original Hogarth lithographs (including that one) on the wall. It's not known where they are now.

★ Notable drinkers in history include: Dr Johnson, George Orwell, Joe Orton, William Hogarth, Charles Dickens and Thomas Paine, one of the founding fathers of the USA. Damian tells American punters that 'your country was born in this pub'.

★ The original Rolo is on the pub's sign outside. People think the pub is named after the dog and come in asking if 'Old Red' is there.

★ There is a theatre upstairs which Kathy Burke and Charlie Hanson (Ricky Gervais's producer on *Derek*, *Extras* and *Life's Too Short*) were instrumental in opening.

★ Judi Dench, Ray Winstone and Daniel Day-Lewis have all performed in the theatre, and theatre punters have included John Hurt and Tim Roth.

40 Buster

THE ALMA, STOKE NEWINGTON, NORTH LONDON

'If someone offered me £1m for him tomorrow, I wouldn't take it.'

Name Buster

Breed King Charles spaniel

Age Three

Owner Wesley Deaton

Buster in three words Cheeky, smiley, flirty.

Loves His ball, and sitting in the window looking outside.

Hates Mice, squirrels, and drunk people. He's wary of them, as if he senses something's wrong.

Locals' favourite Lots of regulars take Buster for a walk. A man who lives across the road and has three kids borrows Buster to play with them in his garden.

Best friend Another King Charles called Louis. There's also a King Charles spaniel (called McNulty) who belongs to a customer – she fancies him, but he's not interested.

Nemesis Sammy, a 'tiny chihuahua thing', they hate each other. Buster runs away though. He's a lover not a fighter.

Unusual habit Stealing socks. In a sort of 'reverse fetch', James has to retrieve them from all around the house. Buster also went through a phase of eating shoes, including an expensive pair of James's Ted Bakers.

Key quote 'If someone offered me £1m for him tomorrow, I wouldn't take it.'

41 Hoppy

Name Hoppy

Breed West Highland terrier

Age Two and a half

Owner Lee Hammerton

Where did you get her? Kent. Her mum lived on a farm.

Hoppy in three words Determined, expressive and silly.

Favourite toys A toy rat, and the classic tennis ball – if she wants to play with her ball she won't take no for an answer.

Best friends She's good friends with Buster from the *Alma*, and a border terrier from Essex.

Nemesis The fox who frequents Lee's back garden.

Her purpose around the brewery Head of security and vermin scarer.

Ever been lost or in danger? She once slipped off the lead getting off the train at their local overland station and bolted. They had no idea where she was running – it turned out she was going straight to the brewery.

Brewery nugget Lee decided to start a brewery in 2014, not knowing that his own family had previously run a 'Hammerton brewery' between 1868 and the 1950s.

GREAT BRITISH PUB DOGS

42 Max

THE WINDMILL, CLAPHAM, SOUTH LONDON

'Such is Max's popularity locally, there has been an outbreak of Bernese mountain puppies being bought in the area.'

Name Max

Breed Bernese mountain dog

Age Three

Owner Ben Evans

Previous owners The family of one of the hotel's receptionists.

Max in three words Bear-like, lazy, cuddly.

Favourite food Max is on an ongoing mission to steal one of the pub's home-made sausage rolls.

Pub dog technique Lounging around looking handsome in the hope of someone giving him a biscuit/sausage roll as a reward. Lots of customers love to stroke him, so he just lies there and lets them get on with it.

Funny habit This dog snores like a train.

Favourite spot Directly beneath the sausage rolls.

Best friend He has a few – Lily the blue Staffy, Minnie the Spanish mastiff and Lola who's a bit of a mix.

Leader of the pack Such is Max's popularity locally, there has been an outbreak of Bernese mountain puppies being bought in the area.

Pub nugget The Windmill is one of Clapham's oldest pubs and backs right on to Clapham Common. In 2016 it was named twenty-third best hotel in the UK by TripAdvisor.

WILLOUGHBY ARMS, KINGSTON, SOUTH-WEST LONDON

Name Holsten

Breed German shepherd

Age Three

Owner Rick Robinson

Reason for name Rick and family wanted the pub dog to be named after a beer, it seemed fitting to go for a German one.

Holsten in three words Loving, soppy, intelligent.

Loves Swimming in the Thames, chasing birds, destroying footballs.

Hates Hi-vis jackets.

Best doggy friend Shady, the Willoughby's other pub dog. Holsten also loves the house cat, Tiggy, but Tiggy couldn't be less interested.

Girlfriend A Great Dane called Techno.

Fun fact Holsten is Facebook friends with Nigel Farage.

Favourite spot The leather sofa under the TV, facing everyone, alongside Shady.

Pub nugget The Yardbirds are said to have rehearsed upstairs in the 1960s, when Eric Clapton was in the line-up. The pub has been the location for two BBC series: *Silk* (Maxine Peake and Rupert Penry-Jones), and *Love Soup* (Tamsin Greig and Olivia Colman).

'The Yardbirds are said to have rehearsed upstairs in the 1960s, when Eric Clapton was in the line-up.'

44 *Coco*

CHANDOS ARMS, COLINDALE, NORTH LONDON

'Some famous musicians have played here over the years, including Ed Sheeran shortly before he was signed.'

Name Coco. Her full name is Coconut Chanel.

Breed Dalmatian

Age Two

Owners Emily and Are Kolltveit

Coco in three words Affectionate, trustworthy, princess-y.

Her previous home All Dogs Matter, a dog charity in nearby Finchley.

Loves Being at Emily's allotment, cuddling on the sofa watching TV, being around people, and most of all, food. Coco is a very creative food burglar.

Hates Being separated from the family, sleeping alone.

Pub dog technique She seeks out the company of customers. She's not that fussy about who.

Favourite food Again, not fussy. Here are some of the things she ate during her first month at the Chandos: an entire loaf of bread fresh out of the oven, all the chocolate from Emily's son's advent calendar, a plastic bag, and the chewing gum off the bottom of the pub tables.

Bad habits Moulting and flatulence.

Walking spots The nearby Montrose Park.

Best friend None in particular but she gets on well with Crunchy (terrier cross) and Lily (Jack Russell).

Pub dog dynasty Prior to Coco there was Mrs Miggins, a chocolate lab, who was synonymous with the pub.

Pub nugget #1 The Chandos Arms was originally built for RAF pilots in World War Two, and has also been a police academy.

Pub nugget #2 Famous musicians have played here over the years, including Ed Sheeran before he was signed, Lee Thompson from Madness, and Jamie Lawson.

Pub nugget #3 When Emily asked the local parish priest to bless the pub when she took it over, he said 'The last time I was here was about seven years ago, and someone was thrown through a window.' The pub has changed somewhat since then.

'The Queen's Head was the inspiration for the Queen Vic in *EastEnders,* as the original writer lived on the square.'

Name Bella

Breed Shih-tzu

Age Nine and a half years

Owner Denise West

Favourite spot Her bed behind the bar.

Best doggy friends Teddy, a chihuahua/ Maltese mix, a randy lad who pushes his way behind the bar to visit her.

Loves Children, other dogs.

Hates Squirrels, pigeons.

Bella in three words Denise's best mate.

What does having a dog bring to a pub 'They're part of pub culture – a good pub should be welcoming and homely and a dog helps with that.'

Scare story As a nipper Bella would run off and was too quick to chase. Not so much these days.

Pub nugget The Queen Mother visited the pub twice, once in the Blitz and again in 1987, when she said the beer was 'much better than champagne'.

46 *Lucky*

THE WINDMILL, BRIXTON, SOUTH LONDON

Name Lucky (nickname 'Roof dog')

Breed German shepherd

Age Five

Owners Seamus McCausland and Kathleen Fleming

Lucky in three words A big puppy.

Loves Destroying footballs.

Hates Small dogs.

Previous pub dogs Lucky followed Ben in 2015, a Rottweiler who became an icon, living at the pub for eight years. Before Ben there were Brandy (Doberman), and Di the yard dog (Alsatian/Rottweiler cross), and many others.

Merch If you like you can drink a pint of Roof Dog beer, then walk away with a Roof Dog T-shirt and badge.

Pub nugget The Windmill is one of the most respected and well-known small music venues in the country.

47 Maxwell and Alfie

THE DUKE, SURBITON, SOUTH-WEST LONDON

'They're spoilt rotten – their food bill is bigger than mine,'
says Alex. 'Max favours rib-eye steak and digestive biscuits.'

Names Maxwell the Great Dane, and Alfie the Victorian bulldog

Ages Maxwell is five, Alfie is ten.

Owner Alex Wells

The names Both dogs were named by the Duke's staff.

The dogs in three words Alfie – stubborn, lazy, loving. Maxwell – gentle, snobby, wimp.

Back story Alfie came from a rescue centre in Dunstable. He'd been found tied up to railings with acid poured on his face. The centre saved his life, and when Alex took him, Alfie was blind and pink from the burn. His vision and swagger have returned in full.

Loves Alfie – putting his arms around people like he's giving you a bear-hug, and hoovering up chips from the floor. Max – his PG Tips monkey toy, and a piece of rope that came off a parcel years ago. They both love riding in Alex's car, especially on the motorway with the roof down.

Hates Max is scared of the following items: tea towels, the Tube, small dogs, bin bags, carrier bags, the washing line, the hoover, and a cardboard cut-out of the Queen.

Style choices Parka for Alfie, Barbour for Max.

Best friends Each other. They go everywhere together and sleep together. Once when Alfie was taken to the vet for an hour, Max trashed the house in protest.

Favourite walks Bushey Park and along the Thames.

Why have resident dogs in the pub?
'It makes you a family pub because dogs make a family. And the place for a dog is definitely a British pub – it's a typical British thing. It's part of the interview for staff: I ask them if they like dogs.'

Pub nugget It's said George Best used to drink at the Duke.

QUINN'S, KENTISH TOWN, NORTH LONDON

PRETTIEST
PUB DOG
AWARD

'The pub has been in the Quinn family for thirty years, and is a rare example of a London pub that's still named after the family.'

Name Rebecca

Breed Rough collie

Age Three

Owners Kevin Quinn and his children Iona, Saoirse and Paidi

Loves Running madly along beaches, as she's very quick and powerful.

Hates Loud noises.

Rebecca in three words Independent, watchful, loyal.

Pub dog technique Around the pub she's a very serene presence. People usually go to her, but she may wander off as she is very independent. Collies have a solitary nature due to their breeding as mountain dogs.

Special move She only responds to commands spoken in French, as she was brought up in Brittany, France. She doesn't understand English commands, no matter how often some people try.

CONQUERING HERO, NORWOOD, SOUTH LONDON

'Defra pays regular visits to the *Conquering Hero* as there are strict rules on keeping a pig, to avoid a foot-and-mouth outbreak.'

Name Frances Bacon

Breed Miniature Vietnamese pot belly/ Gloucestershire old spot cross

Age Six

Owners Victoria and Ian Taylor-Ross

Frances Bacon in three words Affectionate, curious, greedy.

Loves Eating and sleeping.

Hates Getting her trotters clipped ('It's a bit of a wrestle,' says Victoria).

Favourite food/drink Cider and lager because of the sugar, and crunchy food like parsnips, carrots, onion, celery, pineapple, crisps, nuts and the Nurofen out of the barmaid's handbag.

Favourite spot By the fire in winter (she turns herself over to do the other side). In summer she lies under the sofa on her blanket. She also has a pen outside where she goes when food is being served. Wherever she lays her head, she snores.

Great escape Frances Bacon escaped once and tipped over the next-door neighbour's recycling and had a snuffle through.

State surveillance Defra pays regular visits to the Conquering Hero as there are strict rules on keeping a pig, to avoid a foot-and-mouth outbreak. There are checks on Frances Bacon's documents, conditions, diet (pork scratchings are out), and walking routes.

Favourite walk The Defra-approved Norwood Grove. FB loves the crab apples there. As a piglet she would be walked there, now she gets a lift in the car.

Her fellow pets Ripley the Kerry blue terrier, who is deeply suspicious of her, and Taz the cat who is the boss of them all. Taz has been known to sit atop Frances.

Special move Apart from getting up on her hind legs? Getting into Victoria and Ian's bed and putting her head on the pillow as if she were a human. They had to buy extra mattresses to stop this madness.

50 Wellington

THE GREYHOUND, KESTON, BROMLEY, KENT

Name Wellington

Breed Saint Bernard

Time at the pub He lived there his whole life 2013–16

Owners Landlords Toni and Dave Lee

His origins Wellington was a surprise birthday present to Toni from Dave. By the age of three weeks he was already too heavy to carry (Wellington that is, not Dave).

Wellington in three words Big, stubborn, mischievous.

His favourite spot Sprawled out on the floor by the end of the bar, or out the front in the summer by his painting (done by Rosie, who works in the pub). Since Wellington died, the wall with the painting has become the 'Wall of Paws', with small paintings of customers' dogs surrounding Wellington.

Hobbies Journalism – he had a regular column in the pub's monthly newsletter.

Favourite toy Tennis balls. He could get three in his mouth.

Weight 98kg (15½ stone) at his peak. Some dogs would scream when they went into the pub and saw him, before realising he was a massive softie.

Walking spot The woods in Keston.

Loved Toni's mum and brother. He would go berserk for them.

Hated Water. He once jumped in a lake and found he couldn't swim (he had weak back legs). Toni and friend were flat on their faces in the mud, hauling him out.

Naughty habit Stealing sticks off children.

51 *Rudi*

THE MITRE, TWICKENHAM, SOUTH-WEST LONDON

Name Rudi

Breed Show-type cocker spaniel

Age Five months in photos

Owners Chris and Gillian French

Why called Rudi From the Dandy Livingstone song 'A Message to You, Rudy', made famous by the Specials.

Rudi in three words Handsome, funny, adorable.

Favourite food/drink All food, but he has carrots and broccoli at home as treats. He also loves ice cubes and any alcoholic drinks spilt on the floor.

Loves Chasing other dogs in Richmond Park, saying hello to the customers.

Hates He freaks out at the sight of a mop or brush.

Odd habits Sleeping on his back, with everything on show.

Favourite walk Along the river Thames, or Richmond Park.

Pub dog technique Rudi needs no technique. Whoever the customer is, they all seem to love him.

GREAT BRITISH PUB DOGS

Why have a dog in the pub? 'We've always said that the pub is my and Gillian's front room and everyone is welcome. So for Rudi the pub is just like being at home. He's as much a part of the pub now than anyone or anything.'

Pub nugget #1 The pub has a 'Radio 1 On/ Off Air' light box on the wall which Chris and a friend stole from a Fatboy Slim gig they were working at ten years ago. If the pub is 'on air' it's open, and vice versa.

Pub nugget #2 In years gone by the pub had a resident parrot.

Key quote 'We have the best pub dog in the world.'

52 Tully, Reuben and Mathilda

OXYMORON @ THE ROYAL OAK, KENNINGTON, SOUTH LONDON

'The dogs are like family here. They are part and parcel of the pub. Most of the locals just accept their presence.'

GREAT BRITISH PUB DOGS

Name Tully

Breed A 'broken coat' Jack Russell

Age Seven

Owners Lisa and William Hendry

Tully in three words Non-compliant, loyal, fearless.

Favourite toy Tully doesn't do toys.

Favourite spot A customer's lap. Or, if Bill is out, she'll maintain a vigil on the front window ledge.

Love interest Tully has an almost total disregard for boyfriends.

Seasonal hairdo Every spring she grows a Mohican from the top of her head to the tip of her tail – a strip of pure hairy madness that people think is deliberately cultivated by Lisa and Bill.

Top walking spot They all go to the green by the pub where they've got a reputation for being a gang. When things get a bit hot on the green, they head to Archbishop's Park by Lambeth Palace, or to the Thames and its sandy beaches.

Name Reuben

Breed 'Mock Russell' (Jack Russell with some corgi and Alsatian)

Age Five

Behind the name Named after a dog on a TV programme who was a man's only friend on a remote Scottish island.

Reuben in three words Guileless, greedy, good-looking.

Special move Standing on his hind legs, his front paws quivering with the effort of maintaining balance.

Favourite toy A broken tennis ball or a stick as big as a mast.

Love interest Before his libido was torpedoed by 'the op', Reuben was infatuated with a Doberman called India. She was four times his size and only noticed him when she tripped over him going to fetch her ball.

Loves Playing football (his dribbling is better than his passing game).

Hates Fireworks. He will freeze in the corner of the kitchen among the used plastic bags until someone prods him back to life.

Distinguishing marks White hairs on his back from where a mastiff attacked him. He continues to goad larger dogs, but now runs away instead of staying to fight.

Favourite customer For all three of them it's Julian, bringer of high-end dog treats. Reuben also loves playing football with Phil.

Musical accompaniment He howls beautifully when the kids play the recorder or the accordion.

Name Mathilda

Breed Cross of Tully and Reuben, but looks like a classic Jack Russell.

Age Three

Behind the name It was chosen by their son, Hogarth, and probably inspired by the Roald Dahl book.

Mathilda in three words Smart, crazy, lovable.

Favourite toy Anything made of plastic that the children hold dear, Mathilda will chew to death then redistribute via multi-coloured poos.

Love interest Thierry, a long-haired Chihuahua who hops along a bit like she does. He is about the only boy who doesn't get a snarl and a three-legged seeing-off.

Distinguishing marks The lack of a fourth leg. Mathilda was born this way and has developed rhino-strength hind legs which she can stand on for longer than a greedy Reuben.

Taxi service Lisa will often push Mathilda round the park in an old buggy she found at Deptford market. When they reach the soft ground, she tips her out. Lisa concedes she probably has a local reputation for being 'Crazy Pram Dog Woman'.

Why have a resident dog in a pub? 'Because dogs are part of daily life and so are pubs. The two just go together in a particularly British way.'

Their purpose at the Oxymoron? 'To terrify non-dog people and create a space that is lived-in and real. There is a sense of spontaneous, uncontrolled chaos that sets us apart from more formal pubs.'

53 *Crunch*

PRAEWOOD ARMS, ST ALBANS

'His father was a champion basset called California Dreaming.'

Name Crunch

Breed Basset hound

Age Seven

Owner Daniel Redfern

Why called Crunch? His pedigree name is Bassbar Credit Crunch, named after the Hungarian recession, which forced Crunch's intrepid breeder to move back from Hungary to the UK with one hundred unsold basset hounds.

Crunch in three words Loyal, greedy, laid-back.

Favourite spot On the rug by the fire. When he's had enough, he takes himself upstairs to the flat.

Locals' favourite 'People adore him, they laugh at his comical face and ears.' At Daniel's previous pub, the Old Orchard in Harefield, several regulars were so taken with Crunch they bought a basset puppy of their own.

Favourite food On the á la carte menu for Crunch is the free-range chicken with basmati rice; specials are the steak and the lamb shoulder.

Loves A good walk, but he's very slow. The pub holds a regular dog walk of twenty to thirty customers and their dogs. Crunch is always right at the back with the miniature dachshund.

Hates Getting into cars (he doesn't like the motion), the hoover, and balloons.

Claim to fame Crunch had a bit part in TV show *My Life on a Plate*.

Scare #1 A customer's dog once attacked him, tearing his ear off, before another customer came to the rescue. Crunch bravely went under the knife afterwards.

Scare #2 He once fell in the Grand Union Canal in Harefield. He was bending down to drink some delicious canal water, when – being a little top-heavy – he toppled in. To this day, if he encounters a puddle, he has to be lifted over it.

GREAT BRITISH PUB DOGS

'She has her own chair. Some people think she's
a cushion until she moves.'

Name Mellow

Breed Hungarian puli (a type of sheepdog)

Age Ten

Owner Richard Hargroves

Where was she from? A breeder from near
Portsmouth who is a countess. Mellow
arrived with another puli, Missy, who used
to be owned by a member of the Prodigy
(Leroy). Missy passed away in November
2016 aged eighteen.

Mellow in three words Tomboy, friendly,
greedy.

Loves Playing fetch with twigs and
branches. She prefers being in grass to the
forest, where she comes out with brambles
stuck to her.

Hates Having her dreadlocks pulled
(mainly by children).

Scare story When she was two months old,
she ran away from a fireworks party in St
Albans that had 15,000 people in attendance.
Half of them ended up looking for her.

55 *Lizzie*

HORSE AND CHAINS, BUSHEY, HERTS

Name Lizzie

Breed Doberman

Age Seven

Owner Richard Bradshaw Williams

Where from A breeder from Luton. She was the smallest and fell asleep in Richard's wife's arms, so she got picked.

Lizzie in three words Lovable, cheeky, protective.

Favourite food Anything. She goes begging with her doe eyes, and hoovers the floor after closing.

Favourite toy A bear that squeaks, though any cuddly toy will do.

Best friend/love interest She used to have a boyfriend called Shadow – a Doberman who belonged to a customer.

Out and about Her favourite walks are Bushey, Oxhey Park and Merry Hill fields.

Special talent Lizzie is very intuitive and protective of Richard's twin daughters, who are five. When they were babies, if they were crying she would cry too until someone came. She seemed to sense that Richard's wife was pregnant before the couple did.

Pub nugget The earliest reference to the pub was in 1698 when it was known as 'the two cottages at the stump'. Dick Turpin apparently stayed there.

PUMP ROOM BREWERY, HALIFAX, WEST YORKSHIRE

'Fudge eats chicken dumbbells and custard creams.'

Name Fudge

Breed Whippet

Age Six

Owners Tony Holland and Julie Fallows

Fudge in three words Friendly, loyal, unique.

Favourite toy A baby raccoon. She tucks it into bed every night.

Where she walks The moors in Norton Tower, Halifax.

Pub dog dynasty Fudge took over from their previous whippet, Hooch, who died aged sixteen.

Drinks Water over everything, but real ale over lager.

Pub dog technique She very quietly greets all guests when they come in.

Odd habit Burying custard creams (burying is unusual for whippets). Their son Nick also found his missing electric razor in her secret stash in the back garden.

Pub nugget The Pump Room was formerly a café called the Bees Knees which was visited by many a celebrity, including Jarvis Cocker.

57 *Charlie*

MARKET TAVERN, BRIGHOUSE, WEST YORKSHIRE

'The pub was previously a bakehouse where the pies were made for the local butchers.'

Name Charlie

Breed Bichon frise

Age Six

Owners Snap and Deborah Gardner

Charlie in three words Cute, characterful, nuts.

Favourite spot In his basket by the bar.

Loves Running down by the canal and in the local fields around Brighouse. Also, rolling around in snow.

Hates Getting wet. He once walked into what he thought was a puddle, but which turned out to be a big hole in the ground filled with water. He wasn't happy about that. He also has a strong aversion to anyone waving at him.

Pub dog technique Charlie greets every customer with a few barks, then absolutely loses the plot when they try and go. 'He's the perfect pub dog,' said one regular, 'he won't let you leave.'

Best dog friend A Weimaraner who comes in the pub called Boris. Charlie also likes to visit Poppy, the resident black lab at the nearby Cross Keys.

Pub nugget The Market Tavern only opened in February 2016 but has already proved popular. It was previously a bakehouse where the pies were made for the local butchers.

Key quote from Snap 'One of the main reasons we started a pub was me and my wife worked full time and we didn't want to leave Charlie on his own. The pub probably wouldn't even exist if it wasn't for him.' There you have it – the pub dog that existed before the pub.

GREAT BRITISH PUB DOGS

'Delilah joined the team when John gave Della money to go and buy a hoover, and she came back with a Saint Bernard.'

Name Noodle, a Jack Russell/poodle (2003–17)

Noodle in three words Dog in denial (she preferred humans to dogs).

Loved Collecting coins. She had a trick where John would put a penny on his foot and toss it up, then Noodle would catch it and put it back on his foot.

Hated Dogs and children.

Claim to fame Noodle appeared twice on BBC Breakfast. First time was a 'Brexit cook-off' which John appeared in – she tagged along and got on camera. The second time was a second Brexit cook-off that was filmed at the Dog in a Doublet on Brexit referendum day, with John representing England. Again, Noodle made sure she got on telly.

True pub dog Noodle was the face of the pub, and was there from when John and Della took over. RIP Noodle.

Name Delilah, a Saint Bernard aged one

Owners John and Della McGinn

Delilah in three words Big, boisterous, bouncy.

Weight at one year old 76kg (12 stone).

Back story Delilah joined the team when John gave Della money to go and buy a hoover, and she came back with a Saint Bernard.

Loves Hoarding things, eg a bucket of feed that's supposed to be for all the dogs.

Hates Foxes, chickens.

Name Bodie, a boxer/Staffy aged eight

Bodie in three words Daddy's girl, regal.

Pub dog dynasty Bodie's mum was a pure-bred Staffy and a Doublet-er.

Distinguishing features He has one blue eye and one brown one.

Loves His daddy.

Hates Not being near his daddy.

Pub nugget #1 The Doublet is a sixteenth-century building and because of its low-lying position near the river Nene, there have been deaths here over the years, and it has a reputation for being haunted. Not only do the dogs sense it in certain areas of the pub, a contractor stopped working there after a strange incident and a chef quit after two days as he was spooked by the sounds of children running up and down stairs that weren't there.

Pub nugget #2 A 'dog in a doublet' is the bravest dog on a hunt who wears a doublet.

Name Richard, a saluki/greyhound aged one.

Richard in three words Nuisance, needy, loving.

Back story John and Della's daughter was out walking the dogs when a stray followed them home and they decided to keep it. A vet estimated he'd been living wild for about three weeks; he was nicknamed 'Rich le Scritch' as he was skin and bone before they nursed him back to health.

Loves Cuddles, Bodie.

Hates Cars (he was knocked down by one), horses (he was kicked in the chest by one) and bikes (no incident as yet).

59 *Merlin*

KING'S LOCK INN, MIDDLEWICH, CHESHIRE

'A pub seems to make more sense when there's a dog snuggled under the table or by the fireplace.'

Name Merlin

Breed Pointer

Age Two

Owner Dean Elms

The story behind the name He's named after the Merlin brewery in Arclid in Cheshire, one of the pub's main suppliers.

Merlin in three words Silly, lovable, inquisitive.

Favourite food Lamb neck and heart. He also had half a pint of Old Dog from Weetwood Ales for his first birthday.

Favourite toy He finds anything amusing and interactive, even a fallen beer mat can be his favourite toy.

Favourite spot in the bar By the open fire when it's lit.

Best friend Spike, a Labrador/German shepherd cross.

Where does he walk? The local waterways. He also loves the Crosby Beach pointer walk once a month.

How does he interact with the locals? Merlin knows not all locals love dogs, but he soon finds the ones who do.

Why have a resident dog in a pub? A pub makes more sense when there's a dog snuggled under the table or by the fire.

Pedigree heritage His dad, Kiswahili Martin at Kanix, is one of the most decorated English pointers ever shown.

Pub nugget The building was constructed in 1790 to be a toll station for the canal system. The pub today is a free house that has gone anti-brand on all its products.

Bubble and Pip

THE BLUE BELL INN, HALKYN, FLINTSHIRE, NORTH WALES

Names Bubble and Pip

Breed Jack Russell terriers

Ages Thirteen and a half – they're litter mates.

Why the names? Pip has a black spot or 'pip' on her head, and they thought Spot was too masculine. Bubble is very lively!

Bubble and Pip in three words each Pip – canny, quiet, determined. Bubble – bouncy, scatty, willing.

What do they love doing most? Pip loves having her tummy tickled and is canny about making that happen by lying on her back until someone gives in (usually a man). Bubble just loves to play.

Favourite toys There are none. Bubble destroys them all in a matter of seconds.

Favourite spot in the bar In front of the fire, or, especially in the case of Pip, at a customer's feet.

Are there best friends/love interests? No, they live securely under the thumb of the pub cat, Minnie.

Where do they go for walks? On the mountain that starts across the road. When they're out walking, Bubble will paddle in the deepest water while Pip will skirt around the smallest of puddles.

Pub nugget #1 The pub doubles up as the local Post Office branch, after the village PO shut in 2011. It was the second pub in the UK and the first in Wales to do this.

Pub nugget #2 It's purportedly named after a local criminal's boat. Legend has it that he was later caught and hanged for his piracy, and is buried in the nearby Halkyn Castle cemetery.

Pub nugget #3 It was built in the mid-1700s at the crossroads of two old coaching routes.

GREAT BRITISH PUB DOGS

61 *Poppy*

THE SUN TREVOR, LLANGOLLEN, DENBIGHSHIRE, NORTH WALES

Name Poppy

Breed Hungarian vizsla

Age Two

Owners Katy and Paul Jones

Poppy in three words Loving, outdoorsy, energetic.

Favourite spot By the fire.

The outdoor type Whatever activity Katy and Paul are doing, Poppy will join them, whether it's running, cycling, cross-country skiing, open-boat canoeing or converting a barn.

Favourite walks From the pub along the Llangollen canal (a World Heritage Site), or the 'sun bank' walk up to Llangollen's Dinas Bran castle and along to Eglwyseg then back over to the pub.

Pub dog technique She says hello to everybody, loves playing with children, and is a calm presence around elderly people. She's a people dog.

Except? Mike. He's one of the regulars and he accidentally frightened her once in the pub, so now she is freaked out by him.

Food Poppy is allergic to many foods including grain, potatoes, carrots and peas, so she eats raw meat.

62 *Cougar*

DOG AND DUCK, SOHO, CENTRAL LONDON

'He was once stroked by Paul McCartney on Soho Square.'

Name Cougar. 'Zadie's Boy' is his Kennel Club name

Breed Brindle bull mastiff

Age Eleven

Owner Natalie Hubbard

Vital stats 60kg (9½ stone), 71cm (28in) neck.

Cougar in three words Lazy, loyal, gentle.

Loves Unwrapping presents, playing with his squashy ball.

Hates Hats. If someone has a baseball cap on he gets scared and hides behind Natalie.

Claim to fame He was once stroked by Paul McCartney on Soho Square.

His role in the pub Just to be there. He's part of the furniture – everyone knows he belongs to the pub.

Best friends Max at the Crown and Two Chairmen, and Rolo the springer spaniel from the parish church on Soho Square.

Special move #1 Opening crisp packets by whacking his foot on them.

Special move #2 If you are stroking him and then you stop, he lifts half his body up and bashes you to get you to continue, then lies down again.

Special move #3 Trying to get on your knee because he thinks he's small.

Special move #4 If you happen to be clapping about something, he gets overexcited and does a spinning dance and skids around the floor.

Pub nugget The pub is over two hundred years old and is grade-II listed. It takes its name from being in Soho, which was hunting ground at the time. Famous drinkers of the past: John Constable, Dante Gabriel Rossetti and George Orwell, who is believed to have written some of *1984* in there. Madonna has drunk there, but realistically you're more likely to bump into Neil Morrissey or Suggs.

GREAT BRITISH PUB DOGS

63 *Monkey*

SCOLT HEAD, DALSTON, NORTH LONDON

'She likes sitting in the basket on Rosie's bike while she's riding around De Beauvoir.'

Name Monkey

Breed Jack Russell

Age Ten

Owner Rosie Wesemann

Monkey in three words Playful, diva, persistent.

Loves Playing with a lime. She spends much of her time putting a lime at the feet of a customer, then looking up at them till they kick it or throw it away. A stone or cork will also suffice.

Eats Not much now as she is allergic to most things, but her favourite used to be rib-eye steak.

Best doggy friend Poppy, a spaniel/Labrador cross. They often go walking together on Hackney Marshes with Poppy's owner, Maureen.

Favourite people in the pub Jackie the general manager (who is the only person Monkey will sit quietly with on the sofa), and Sylvester the chef.

Special move Sitting in the basket on Rosie's bike while she rides around De Beauvoir.

64 *Pearl*

ROSEMARY BRANCH, HAGGERSTON, NORTH LONDON

'Obstinate, dominant and demanding...'

Name Pearl

Breed Miniature schnauzer

Age Seven

Owner Lucie Marshall

Pearl in three words Obstinate, dominant and demanding.

Favourite spot In the green tub chairs.

Best friend There are dozens who come into the pub, but the main canine is Pippa, a rescue collie cross.

Loves Chasing ducks and swans, and scouring the floor for pork scratchings.

Hates The hoover and fireworks.

Favourite walk Botany Bay and Margate beach.

Favourite food Sardine and sweet potato fish cakes, cooked by Lucie.

PEARL PICTURED IN 2017 (OPPOSITE) AND IN 2010 (ABOVE).

Pearl is best known for Her jumpers. She has a Where's Wally one, a bee one, and a mustard one, all cable-knit.

Special move She pees like a boy dog, cocking her leg up against every tree on her walks.

Scare story Pearl once went missing and Lucie had the entire pub out looking for her. It turned out she'd been upstairs at the pub's small theatre – she had gone in after the interval for the second half, and was hiding down behind the stage. She eventually got bored of the show and trotted across the stage as a sort of canine heckle.

65 *Ronnie*

THE GLAD, BOROUGH, SOUTH LONDON

Name Ronnie, named after Ronnie Lane, Dan's hero.

Breed Border terrier

Pub dog tenure 2009–11

Owner Dan Orcese

Ronnie in three words Aloof, tough, energetic.

Loved Music – The Glad was a music pub (it closed in 2016) and sometimes Ronnie watched the bands right in front of the bass drum. Trumpets and violins were no problem for Ronnie. He also loved being affectionate to his close coterie of friends and colleagues. Preferred women to men.

Musical tastes He preferred the more mellow, acoustic stuff.

Hated Suitcases with wheels on, and most other dogs (outside the pub).

Distinguishing features He had an extra thumb on both front paws.

Role in the pub He was general manager. 'Sometimes I think I worked for him,' says Dan.

Pub dog technique Largely aloof, but would accept strokes. Those he truly trusted, he would sit next to and gradually press himself against them.

Walking spots The Thames at low tide was his favourite, as it was so quiet.

Key quote 'One of the regulars said he's like a great war colonel, with his whiskers and his demeanour.'

Name George

Breed Black Labrador

Age Eleven

Owner Matt Ward

Favourite spot He has his own chair. If there's someone sitting there, he politely suggests that they move on.

George in three words 'My best mate.'

Loves The sea. Especially at Whitstable.

Hates Fireworks. He has the dog equivalent of Prozac for it, as it's getting worse with age. Christmas crackers are increasingly becoming a problem too.

His role in the pub He's a shared dog and lots of locals ask if they can take him for a walk. People notice if he's not in the pub.

Favourite food Chicken. George has been known to leave the pub and loiter around outside the local chicken shops.

Walkies George's regular walks are around Hilly Fields and Brockwell Park.

Scare story While Matt was away at a wedding, a customer took George for a walk in Brockwell Park where the Lambeth Country Fair was happening. Matt never found out whether the fair's famous Chucklehead cider played a part in the disappearance, but George ended up wandering off and was found in Streatham.

CROWN AND TWO CHAIRMEN, SOHO, CENTRAL LONDON

'Max and the pub have welcomed the likes of George Clooney, Jude Law … and of course, Suggs.'

GREAT BRITISH PUB DOGS

Name Maxwell

Breed Bearded collie

Age Ten

Owners Craig Livingstone and Shaun Athey

Max in three words Fun-loving, noisy, happy.

Favourite spot In front of the bar or in the corner on the red sofa.

Loves Big walks, going into the bushes for a scratch. He also loves the regulars – like Eddie who comes in at noon every day with his King Charles spaniel, and Natalie and Cougar from the nearby Dog and Duck.

Hates Much like Cougar, people wearing hats are his *bête noir*. Max is also not keen on people greeting each other or showing affection, as it's his pub and he should get all the attention.

Favourite places to walk Most of the big central London parks: Green Park, Regents Park, Primrose Hill and Hyde Park.

Famous friends Max and the pub have welcomed the likes of George Clooney (his is a Guinness), Jude Law, Leigh Francis (a friend of Craig and Shaun's from Leeds), Vernon Kaye, and of course, Suggs.

Scare story They were on a narrowboat in Uxbridge, and Craig had gone on land while another boat went through the lock. Max tried to jump across the gap to get to Craig, but misjudged it and fell into the rapidly dropping water. Luckily he wasn't hurt.

Why have a resident dog in a pub?
'It makes it like a country pub in central London.'

Pub nugget The name is said to come from the days of Queen Anne, who would get her portraits done on Dean Street, where the pub is. Her chair carriers would go into the local hostelry for a drink, and the name was born.

HASSOCKS HOTEL, HASSOCKS, WEST SUSSEX

'The gang go nuts for a camping holiday and a day at the beach, swimming and running around.'

Names Ochre, Rufus, Rosie and Ruby

Breed Red setter

Ages Nine (all from the same litter of twelve).

Owners Gillian Lamb, Joanna Greenhalgh.

Ochre in three words Shy, loving, faithful.

Rufus in three words Laid-back, greedy, loving.

Rosie in three words Bossy, loyal, social.

Ruby in three words Scatty, affectionate, soppy.

Pub dog dynasty Until 2016, Hassocks was also home to Ember, mother to all four of the current lot.

Dynamic Rosie has taken the role of mum since Ember died (Gillian and Joanna say they always knew this would be the case). The three girls tend to stick together.

Twin brother Another of the litter won the 'puppy setter' category at the 2012 Crufts.

Group activities The gang go nuts for a camping holiday and a day at the beach, swimming and running around. They especially like Norman's Bay near Eastbourne.

Ochre's tastes She loves liver, running, and truffling in nearby Butchers Wood. She hates shiny floors, congestion and loud noises.

Rufus's tastes He loves pinching food, especially Peperami. He hates being woken up when he's on the sofa, and having his ears touched.

Rosie's tastes She adores her family, and doesn't like it when someone blows on her face.

Ruby's tastes She loves getting all the cuddles, all the time. She presses up against people for body contact. She hates balloons, and even wee'd herself once when she was a puppy as she was so scared.

Their purpose in the pub 'They're a pet dog for all sorts of people who can't have one themselves. Some people are scared of dogs, and we've had many people change their mind after meeting the setters.'

Pub nugget The Clayton tunnel crash in 1861 was the worst British train accident at the time, and the pub cellar was used as a temporary mortuary. The dogs happily go down there, which suggests it's not haunted.

Name Twiglet

Breed Puggle (pug/beagle cross)

Age Three

Behind the name It was a toss-up between Twiglets and Quavers as to which pub snack she would be named after.

Twiglet in three words Robust, loving, child-friendly.

Favourite walk The local farm passes and around the village.

Loves Chasing deer.

Twiglet and the setters 'They're all just best mates. She was a puppy when they were all seven years old, now they all hang out together. She even sleeps on top of them.'

Competition winners

We asked our Twitter and Instagram followers at @pubdogsgb to send in their pub dog photos – thank you for all your entries, here are our lucky winners!

SACHA, SIBERIAN HUSKY, AT THE RED LION INN, EPWORTH, DONCASTER

BILLY LAMB CHOPS, JACK RUSSELL, AT THE FESTIVAL PUB, COVENTRY

JACK, BLACK LABRADOR, AT THE MALLARD, LYNEHAM, WILTSHIRE

MAX, BICHON FRISE, AT THE ALBION, FARNHAM, SURREY

JAZZ, DELPHI BEAN, AND SHISHKA, POINTERS, AT THE BELL INN, CASTLE HEDINGHAM, ESSEX

MURPHY, COCKER SPANIEL, THE TOBIE NORRIS, STAMFORD

TANIS, LABRADOODLE, AT THE VICTORIA INN,
CARRONSHORE, FALKIRK

LUCIA, BLUE GREAT DANE, ALSO AT THE BELL
INN, CASTLE HEDINGHAM, PICTURED IN 1991

HARRY, BLACK LABRADOR AT THE
ST KEW INN, CORNWALL

JAKE, SPRINGER SPANIEL, AT THE RED LION,
BONVILSTON, VALE OF GLAMORGAN

LUDO, LABRADOODLE, AT THE OLD NUN'S HEAD,
SOUTH LONDON

LUNA, ITALIAN SPINONE, AT THE THREE TUNS
IN BUNTINGFORD, HERTS